Dali & His Doctor

The Surreal Friendship Between Salvador Dali and Dr. Edmund Klein

By Paul Chimera
Copyright 2016

To Anne, Catherine, Kristy, Joe, Carolyn, my parents (Mary and Joseph), Cassie, Carrie, Martha Klein and the entire Klein family, and to the late, great Dr. Edmund Klein and Salvador Dali.

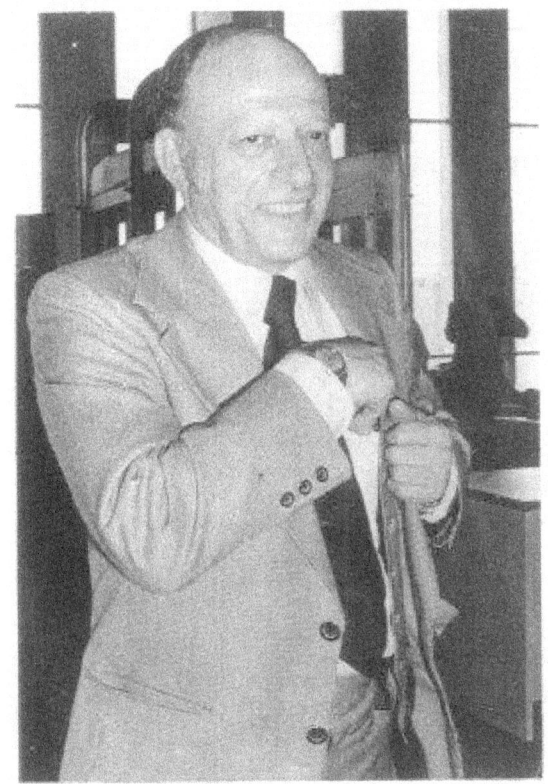

Dr. Edmund Klein

Table of Contents

CHAPTER 1

Phone Call Leads to Enduring Friendship

There's no better word than *surreal* to describe the moment. "Dali's manager phoned the house," recalls Martha Klein, widow of renowned dermatologist Dr. Edmund Klein, "and announced, 'Salvador Dali calling for Dr. Klein...'"

It wasn't exactly the kind of call one receives every day.

There was no introduction or explanation needed. When a man in a Spanish accent telephones all the way from Europe – in 1972, long before cell phones -- to say Surrealist artist Salvador Dali is calling, one tends to sit up and take notice.

That man was Enrique Sabater, who was the celebrated artist's personal manager at the time. He followed Peter Moore's tenure in that role, and preceded Dali's third and last manager – long-time friend and Dali author/photographer, Robert Descharnes.

And so it began. A long-distance phone call that would ignite a seemingly improbable relationship between two extraordinary men: Salvador Dali, world-famous painter-genius; and Dr. Edmund Klein, renowned dermatologist, skin cancer researcher, and medical pioneer, who counted the likes of actor John Wayne and even U.S. President Lyndon Baines Johnson among his patients.

As best anyone can tell (doctor/patient confidentiality precludes a definitive answer), Dali had developed a significant skin disorder, most likely cancer or a precancerous condition. He and his wife Gala lived most of their life on Spain's Costa Brava. Dali spent many hours under the sometimes unforgiving sun – painting, fashioning objets d' art, or receiving guests and regaling them with wild tales or silly or sexy surrealist reveries. It's not a huge leap to suspect that Dali's long-time exposure to the sun's damaging rays may have led to some health problems.

Whatever medical condition Dali eventually developed, it was clearly skin-related and serious enough to enlist someone with Dr. Edmund Klein's expertise. There can be little doubt that when Dali's Andorra-based manager, Enrique Sabater, was tasked with finding the best skin cancer expert in the world to attend to the most prominent artist in the world, he did due diligence in locating the best man for the job.

Martha Klein believes Mary Lasker also may have had a hand in leading Sabater and Dali to Dr. Klein's doorstep in Williamsville, New York, a Buffalo suburb. Lasker was an American health activist and philanthropist who raised funds for medical research and created the Lasker Foundation. She was a friend of both the Klein's and the Dali's. Indeed, Dali executed a portrait of Ms. Lasker, and Dr. Klein would go on to receive the coveted Albert Lasker Award in 1972 – the most prestigious honor in American medicine – for his pioneering work in developing treatments for premalignant and malignant skin cancers.

The esteemed Lasker Award, presented on November 16, 1972 and hand-signed by Mary Lasker, President, and Sidney Farber, Chairman, read in part: *Dr. Klein's pioneering and persistent efforts have extended, to an important degree, the therapeutic attack on cancer. For his outstanding contribution this Albert Lasker Medical Research Award in Clinical Cancer Chemotherapy is given."*

The irony of this strange union – a dermatologist in Buffalo and a famous Surrealist master from Catalonia – was not lost on those who knew both men. Six degrees of separation can sometimes forge unlikely unions.

But was it really that improbable? Maybe not. In fact, those who knew Dr. Klein well – his wife, of course (Mary Alice Doble and Edmund married on Oct. 25, 1952); his children (two of whom are physicians) his patients and others – knew he was, on some level, an intense and sometimes eccentric man. His passion for his work was beyond palpable. His genius as a physician and researcher was borne out by exceptional accomplishments.

And in the other corner – Salvador Dali. Need we say more? A titan of twentieth century art. A showman whose flamboyance and public eccentricities, along with that outrageous mustache, were perhaps more famous than his remarkable paintings, drawings and sculptures.

And so, as fate would have it, two giants in their respective fields became fast friends. *Dali & His Doctor* tells the story behind the Dali/Klein pairing, and the fascinating personal collection of Dali drawings, sketches and objects that resulted from their unique friendship. Like Dali and Dr. Klein, the collection itself would go on to world-wide recognition – revealed to the world after decades in complete seclusion.

*   *   *   *   *

To say Edmund Klein was no ordinary doctor, no ordinary man, may sound trite or cliché. But the evidence is undeniable: he was indeed an exceptional individual whose personal story arcs its way from tragedy to triumph.

This was a man who literally found the cure for cancer. At least a form of it. In the 1984 book, "The Book of Jewish Lists," author Ron Landau included a section called "The World's Fifty Most Important Jews (1974)." Listed, among others, were goliaths of their age: Leonard Bernstein, Conductor; Marc Chagall, Artist; Henry Kissinger, Diplomat; and Edmund Klein, Developer of a cancer treatment.

And, like Salvador Dali — while busy being a genius — Dr. Klein also managed to ruffle a few feathers along the way.

In his *New York Times* obituary (July 30, 1999), for instance, the newspaper noted: "Dr. Klein found himself amid controversy in 1977, when he was interviewed by a *Reader's Digest* writer for an article about skin cancer in general and stated 'authoritatively' that President Lyndon B. Johnson had been treated for it. Although President Johnson had died four years earlier, the report was considered significant, not so much because of the seriousness of the illness as because of the implication of secrecy previously surrounding the President's condition."

The *American National Biography* online (www.anb.org) reported on the incident this way: "In the post-Watergate era in which the story appeared, the allegations of a secret medical cover-up in the White House proved irresistible to the media. Although Klein claimed to have been authorized by a member of Johnson's family to disclose the facts, he declined to name his source, and both the Johnson family and the former physicians flatly denied the story, admitting only that Johnson had been treated for a skin condition of lesser severity."

Any indiscretion aside, however, the central story of Dr. Klein is one of almost limitless achievement. In attempting to summarize the accomplishments of the man who earned the moniker, "the father of immunotherapy," the *Journal of the American Academy of Dermatology (Vol. 44 No. 4, 2001)* included in list form (and abridged here):

1. The invention with Dr. Djerassi of the closed systems of plastic bags for the sterile separation of whole blood into its components of plasma, red blood cells, platelets, and white blood cells.
2. The first biomedical research on the effects of laser working in animals with Samuel Fine, before others did so in humans.
3. Local antitumor chemotherapy for neoplastic cutaneous lesions, for which he received the Lasker Award. He developed topical 5-fluorouracil therapy, an anticancer treatment still approved by the Food and Drug Administration and available commercially.
4. Discovering the value of immunotherapy for cutaneous

cancers and thus pioneering modern immunotherapy.

5. Early work in clinical exploration of lymphokines in patients with neoplastic disease, which led to today's preeminence of cytokines and interleukins. He first demonstrated that administration of lymphokines to accessible tumors in humans can result in regression of malignant diseases.

6. Devising low-dose vinblastine therapy for Kaposi's sarcoma, one of the earliest effective treatment methods for this neoplasm.

The publication followed the above list with these simple and telling words: "Edmund Klein was an amazing person. His interests were legion. He worked long, and sometimes very odd, hours...." Those wide-ranging interests included his eventual connection with Dali, as it was noted in the *Journal of Medicine*, Vol. 30, Nos. 5&6, 1999: "There was more to Ed Klein, the man...We will never forget watching him evaluate patients at almost midnight, speaking with them while leaning upon his glass covered Salvador Dali masterpiece stretched out on his consultation room desk...."

The internet's encyclopedia, Wikipedia, notes that Dr. Klein "developed a technique that allowed the separation of whole human blood into its component parts of plasma, platelets, white blood cells, and red blood cells, greatly increasing the efficiency of the entire transfusion process; now three people could benefit from a single donor instead of one, with red blood cells used for anemic individuals, platelets for cancer patients, and plasma for those with decreased blood volume. Klein's results were published in both the New England Journal of Medicine and the Journal of Pediatrics and earned him the first prize for originality of research from the International Society of Hematology in 1956."

In 1962, Dr. Klein was testing some drugs against skin cancer, when one patient displayed a serious allergic reaction. By reducing the concentration of the allergy-producing material, the tumor disappeared. In the book, "The Miracle Finders" by Donald Robinson, the author said of Dr. Klein's success in this case, "This was not chemotherapy at work. It was the first demonstration of the immune system's capacity to vanquish cancer.

"'For the first time,' Dr. Klein testified to a committee of the U.S. Senate, 'we were able to take the cause of a disease, namely allergy, and turn it into a therapeutic weapon. We are able to take it out of the hands of the devil and put it into the hands of God.'"

Born Oct. 22, 1922, in Vienna, Austria, Edmund Klein would one day become personal physician to Salvador Dali. And lay claim to many other extraordinary accomplishments along the way. He was the son of a Viennese cantor, and would obtain a British visa that put him in England in 1938 in time to narrowly escape the Anschluss. He arranged the flight from harm's way of his sister, Ruth, too (she lived in England all her life, until her death in 2014), but the same fortunes didn't bless his parents; sadly, they could not be persuaded to leave their homeland.

As *The Journal of the Academy of Academic Dermatology* noted, "This Viennese-born, British-, Canadian-, and American-educated physician received an amazing total of 36 scholarships for academic proficiency." Klein launched his academic medical research career at the University of Toronto Medical School, Toronto, Ontario, Canada, receiving his M.D. degree under the direction of Dr. Charles H. Best, co-discoverer of insulin, in 1951. He did additional research with Sidney Farber and others at Harvard Medical School and completed a dermatology residency at Massachusetts General Hospital.

Following medical school, Klein served as a research fellow at Harvard University and then as a research associate at the Children's Medical Center in Boston, Massachusetts from 1952 to 1958. He was appointed assistant professor of dermatology and medicine at Tufts University School of Medicine in 1959.

Martha Klein shared with me something of the emotional impact her husband's work had on him. "Edmund got a fellowship to go to Harvard and he worked a few years at the Sidney Farber Jimmy Fund Building. He worked on children with leukemia, and that was heartbreaking. During that time, we had a terrible polio outbreak as well. I think he suffered a burn-out after a while. It was such a terrible emotional drain. He decided to go to the Mass. General in a residency in dermatology. It is ironic, because he ended up working on malignancies of the skin."

*   *   *   *

A few years later, Klein became affiliated with the prestigious Roswell Park Memorial Institute (known today as Roswell Park Cancer Institute) and in 1961 became research professor and chairman of Roswell's Department of Dermatology, devoting some twenty-five years to his life's calling. One of Dr. Klein's most important innovations was his creation of an intravenous therapy for Kaposi's sarcoma that featured low dosages of vinblastine. This proved to be one of the first effective treatments of a cancer "that gained increasing prominence as the AIDS epidemic unfolded," according to the American National Biography online. Dr. Klein served as a member of the National Advisory Council on Health Care Technology at the Department of Health & Human Services, and he frequently testified before Congress as an advocate of increased cancer research funding.

Dr. Klein's widow, Martha shared with me a document her husband dictated to her just before he died in 1999. "He had already had many mini-strokes," Martha notes. This extraordinary and poignant bit of history, which Dr. Klein titled "Vienna, Only You Can Be the City of My Dreams," is herein reproduced in its entirety:

The title of this book is taken from a favorite Viennese song, 'Vienna, City of My

Dream.' Most of what I am going to say will describe the downfall of 'The City of My Dreams,' to the City of My Nightmares.

Until 1918, this is until end of the first World War, Vienna was the capital of a country containing over 60 million people. As part of the peace treaty of Versailles, the Austrian Empire was divided into a series of independent states. Vienna, however, retained the multiple national character that it had acquired during the imperial period of Austria. On the other hand, Austria in part and Vienna almost in total, became a social democratic entity, leading to the nickname of 'RED VIENNA' during the early 1920s. However, despite the liberal façade, implied by the social democratic government of Vienna, Vienna remained, or became more nationalistic than it had been during its imperial state. In the course of its nationalism, Vienna became even more anti-Semitic than it had under the emperor.

The Austria-Hungarian Empire was divided into a number of independent states or parts of pre-existing national states. The Balkan provinces of Austria, Croatia, Bosnia and Herzegovina formed Yugoslavia. Since the middle of the thirteenth century, Austria was ruled by the Hapsburgs, a Swiss noble family that was elected by the electoral princes, including the Archbishop of Cologne, Mienst and Trier, who selected the Hapsburg patriarch, Rudolph Von Hapsburg, as a successor to the dukes of Austria. The dynasty of Babenberger was without a future heir. Austria gradually acquired control of Hungary, Bessarabia (now part of Romania), Czechoslovakia, Galicia (now part of Poland), Croatia, Bosnia and Herzegovina (now part of Yugoslavia). Also following the Treaty of Versailles, Austria ceded the southern part of Tyro, one of its federated states. Southern Tyro and particularly its largest and most popular city, Meran, remained one of the reasons for discord between Italy and Austria, and subsequently Germany.

Austria, even though it was not necessarily the most popular part of the Austria-Hungarian Monarchy, managed to exert political, as well as military control, where there was resistance. My own family represented an example of the multinational character than ended up in Vienna. My mother came from Galicia, now part of Poland, and my father came from a Jewish background in Hungary.

I cannot recall any indication of discord, based on national origin between my parents. My father, however, suffered from a disease that seemed to force him to give away part of his income every month to people that he said were worse off than we. In fact, in retrospect, it seems to me that my father knew more people that did not have enough to eat than anyone else I had ever heard of. The only disagreement that I was aware of between my parents was my mother's objection to my father's generosity, which seemed excessive and I would tend to agree with her.

My mother's family was closely knit and had all the characteristics of a Polish Jewish family; i.e., fairly close adherence to Jewish religious ritual; closeness between siblings; she has three brothers and one sister. My mother was gentle, yet firm, and delicate. She and her sister were on close terms. Her sister, Ruth, being financially better off than we, paid annually for our trips to Krakow (today's Poland) and for vacations in the country. The vacations were modest; we rented a room or two from a peasant, who was usually not in the house that we were renting. The country places that we went to for the bulk of our vacations were usually no more than an hour from Krakow. We went there by train in order to have frequent contact with the folks in the family; at times their children joined us, under my mother's supervision to have a vacation along with us.

Austria, which had shrunk to a country of six million people from the Austria-Hungarian Empire that had contained more than sixty million people, was predominantly Catholic (more than 90%). In close circles, it was frequently suggested that the Cardinal Archbishop of Vienna, and that of Saltsburg, ruled Vienna and in a sense this was true. Certainly nothing would be done without their consent if it hadn't indeed already been originated by the two Archbishops in the first place. One of the reliable messages that was transmitted or at least allowed to be perpetuated from generation to generation was that the Jews killed Christ. This patently untrue message was one of the roots of the anti-Jewish attitude of the Austrians. The fact that two thousand years had elapsed since the apparent death of Jesus did not seem to mitigate the furor of the Christians and Jews in Austria.

My father's family was less cohesive. My paternal grandfather lived in Vienna. He was an orthodox Jew (a Chasid) who still observed the Jewish rite of ear locks that were never cut. My father had three brothers, the oldest of whom lived in Vienna and occasionally came to visit us. Two other brothers lived in Germany (in

Berlin). One of them had two sons and the other one had no children. My father's brother who lived in Vienna had a daughter who was a teenager when I met her.

Germany was already under National Socialist (Nazi) rule. Jews in Germany had already started to leave (mainly to the U.S. and S. America). One evening when I stayed over at a friend's house for dinner, the boy's father told us that he had recently come back from a visit to Germany. He said that following a recent trip by the British Foreign Sec. (Eden) the rumor was that he had made an agreement with the German government that would allow it to occupy Austria. I became very upset about what he said and decided at that point to get out of the country and to a place where there were no Nazi's. Even though the National Socialist party was illegal in Austria, many Austrians joined the underground where National Socialists were not only prominent but were in the vast majority. My parents like most other Jews in Austria had no foreboding and thought that I was being childishly and immaturely alarmed.

The Anschluss, the taking over of Austria by Germany, brought an immediate change. It was not safe to walk on the street because Nazi party members such as the Brown Shirts (S.S.A.) and the black uniformed S.S. guards were ubiquitous and reputed to pick Jews up off the streets and send them to concentration camps in Germany.

Before the Anschluss, I had written to several schools in England (*editor's note: Edmund was 16 at the time*) and the headmaster of one of them sent me a letter stating that my grades were such that I could be admitted to the last year of high school there. He did not raise the question of how I would live, where I would stay, etc. I went to the British Consulate with the letter and the clerk at the desk said that it was a good letter, but then raised all the pertinent questions for which I had no answer. But the British consulate was a place in which I felt very comfortable, and knew that no one could pick me up there and send me to a concentration camp.

However, I realized if I just stood in the hallway someone would eventually ask me what I was doing there, so I walked around and I saw a little room off the main hallway and 6 or 7 people were standing there in front of the doorway. Each of them had a briefcase in their hands, presumably with documents and I thought to myself, I have a document too. I had a letter from a school in England so I folded it carefully and held it under my arm. I was the last in line. Then the door opened and a middle-aged rather heavy-set man spoke to each of the people in front of me and presumably arranged another time when he would see them, and then he came to me, or that I came to him, and I carefully unfolded the letter that I had and showed it to him.

He looked at it briefly and said, "Ok, where is your passport?" I said, "I'm sorry, I don't have a passport with me." He said, "Well then, how can I give you a visa if you don't have a passport?" I said, "Well, I'll try to get a passport as quickly as possible," and then I had a brilliant idea. I said, "Maybe if you can give me a letter saying there is a visa to Britain awaiting the issuance of a passport, it might speed up the process." He nodded his head, stepped back to his desk (a massive old desk), sat down and called his secretary.

He dictated "To Whom It May Concern: Edmund Klein has a visa to go to Britain pending the issuance of a passport. Yours truly" and then an illegible signature. He said, "When you have a passport, come back and see me gain." I said, "Whom shall I say I am coming to see?" He said, "Tell them you are coming to see Captain Kenrick, the chief of the passport office." I almost jumped six feet.

This meant that I might go to England even though I did not know how I would eat or where I would live, etc. I went home and two months later I received my passport. I went back to the British Consulate. When I got there the building was surrounded by a line of people waiting to get into the consulate. Captain Kenrick arrived at the consulate in a chauffeur-driven limousine. I followed the limousine after he got out, thinking that perhaps I could enlist the help of the chauffer. I put a ten shilling note in my passport along with the letter from Capt. Kendrick, stating that I had a visa to go to England. The chauffeur pocketed the ten shilling note and took the letter and my passport and disappeared into the consulate. Those were the longest moments of my life.

I was worried that I had let the passport out of my hands and wondered if I would ever get it back. I thought I was foolish to let the documents out of my sight. But in about ten minutes the chauffeur came back with my things and showed me that a visa had been issued. At this point, I asked the chauffer if he could arrange for me to get into the consulate so that I could personally thank Captain Kenrick and ...(original document's transition here unclear)....the visa to you. I said, "Yes, I know and I want to thank you," and he said. "Do you still have the letter from the principal in England?" I said, "Yes, it's right here," and I pulled it out and handed it to him. He scribbled a note at the bottom of the letter which was totally illegible, so I don't know what it said, but he said, "Look, if you have any trouble when you get to England with immigration show them this letter." Then he shook my hand and told me he wished me the best of luck.

My mother brought me some clothes in the expectation that I would not be able to buy any once I got to England. The ticket was by railroad through Germany into Belgium and then on to Dover. My mother took me to the train and that is the last time I saw her.

I didn't want her to go into danger but she insisted, saying she may never see me again. I was on the train within two or three days and on my way to England. At the border of Germany and Belgium everybody had to get off the train with their luggage to be examined by S.S.

guards. This was to see if anyone was trying to smuggle money, gold or jewelry out of the country. I was lucky that my suitcase was examined early and as heavy as it was I ran to get on the train just as it was leaving. Hundreds of people had been on the train and very few were allowed back.

At the next stop, the black-shirted Nazis got off the train and very quickly got on another train heading back to Germany. In the compartment in which I was sitting there were five Belgians who were congratulating me and were in general jovial except for one. He sat stiff-faced and did not bother to speak to me. I was in Belgium, a free country, and I said to him, "Vous es un Degrell." Degrell was the leader of a fascist party in Belgium. He said, "No, No, No," but the other passengers in the compartment started to snicker at him and laugh and from this I gathered that I had been right in my assessment of him. The train went to the British Channel and then I went onto the ferry, the Dover Ferry. The immigration official at Dover asked me all the questions for which I had no answer. For example, "Where will you stay?" and "How will you pay for your food?" At this point I picked out the letter from Captain Kendrick and showed it to him. He said, "Will you give me that letter?" and I said, "No, I don't think I can."

At this point he nodded his head and pointed toward the entrance that was for British citizens and for those whose papers are in order. I started to walk toward that entrance and suddenly heard the official calling me back. My heart stood still for a minute. I walked back and the man said to me, "You know if you had given me that letter I would not have let you into England."

I was now in England with an intense feeling of joy along with a feeling of sad apprehension. Where was I going to go when I arrived in London? I did have a letter from a classmate that had gone to England before me. I went to his place and just moved in but about a week later the people with whom he lived moved out and took Eric, my friend, with them. Evidently Eric's mother had found a way to send him money on a regular basis. I remained in the empty house, sleeping on my suitcase. Another occupant, who lived in the basement of the house, was a woman in her late thirties who lived there with her daughter who was about 18 or 19. The woman, the mother, was very heavily made up and wore very flirty clothes and since she was gone overnight almost every night I came to the conclusion that she was probably a prostitute. Nevertheless, she occasionally gave me food which I of course accepted, but I felt strange about this, a little like a pimp perhaps.

There was a private street in the vicinity and on that street there were several houses that were particularly impressive. At one of these I used to linger. There were gates at each end of this private street and people had keys to lock and unlock the gate so that they could drive in and out. There was one house in particular that I liked. It was very beautiful and I would stand and just look at it, fascinated with it. I used to think how nice it would be if I could stay in one of them. One day when I was standing, looking at the house, a chauffeured limousine pulled up and entered the circular driveway in front of the house. A man got out of the car and the car pulled up to the entranceway of the driveway where I was standing. The chauffeur got out of the car and asked me what I was doing there and I said that I just liked to look at the house. He asked a few questions about who I was and where I came from and then he got back into the car and drove back up to the entrance.

He then came back with the man I had seen get out of the car and he also asked me a few questions, including my name, where I lived, etc. and then got back into the car. The car returned to the house. That same afternoon when I came back to the empty house where I was staying, a man, the chauffeur, came up to me and introduced me to a lady who was sitting in the back of the car. She said, "Can you get your things down?" I said, "Yes, I have three suitcases," and she told the chauffeur to help me get the suitcases down and put them into the car and then she said, "I saw the woman who lives downstairs and I don't know what you are doing in the company of people like that."

We were off to the beautiful house that I had so much admired. The woman said that her name was Mrs. Friedland and that she and her husband had decided to give me a place to stay until more permanent arrangements could be made for my living conditions. During this time I received a letter from my mother. She had found the name of two distant relatives who lived in London and she thought they might be willing to help me.

One was a Dr. Freeder, who was a professor at the London School of Economics. I did get in touch with him and he was not particularly pleased to see me or hear from me. But he said that he had a former student who was now governor of New Zealand and he would get in touch with him to see if he could get me a permit to go to New Zealand. The other relative was a Mrs. Hausenball, whom I called for an appointment, but she was always too busy to see me. She sounded like a typical British career woman. She finally agreed to see me at the Woburn House, a center that had been set up to handle the refugee problem. She asked me if I would not be better off just going back to Germany and staying with my parents. At this point I told her that I had seen Dr. Freeder and that he had a student who was now governor of New Zealand and that he thought I might get a permit to go to New Zealand. She waved her hand impatiently and said, "Who knows when that might be done if it even happens at all." I was beginning to think that the student and governor of New Zealand might be just fiction, just to keep me from fighting a return to Germany by diverting my attention.

I did go back to see Dr. Freeder and he said he had not heard anything and then he said the same thing that Mrs. Hausenball had said. "Don't you think you would be best off to just go back? Where are you staying so that I can get in touch with you?" At this point I started to get quite suspicious and decided not to tell him anything. I said I am living on the streets and I sleep on park benches. He replied, "Well, that is too bad." At this time I turned and left and never saw either of these distant relatives again. I stayed with the Friedlands for five or six weeks until Mrs. Freidland told me some friends had expressed a desire to meet me and were considering giving me a place to stay with them. I didn't know how to take this news. The thought of leaving this house upset me a great deal.

During the time that I stayed at the Friedlanders, the British government, in a move of compassion, passed an immigration rule, admitting children under 20 years of age, without any means of support, to enter England. I decided to offer my services to the committee. I was hoping to find a sponsor for my younger sister, Ruth. No sponsor seemed to be forthcoming, until one day I happened to see a paper in a wastebasket. On that paper I found the name and address of a person interested in supporting a teenager. His name was Harry Heading.

Upon inquiry, I was told that he was a gangster and not an appropriate sponsor. Nevertheless I thought a gangster was better than a Nazi. I looked into it further. Harry Heading lived in an affluent part of London. I went to his place and when I went into the lobby two rough-looking men were standing by the elevator. When I got to the floor, another two men were waiting as I exited the elevator. They checked me out as well but had evidently been expecting me. I went into Harry Heading's apartment. Harry Heading was thin, of medium height and had a baby face but was probably in his mid- to late-thirties. He asked me to show him the forms that I had filled out for my sister from the committee. He looked at the information about my sister and he said, "No, we won't be going back to the committee. We will do this in a different way."

He picked up the phone and called someone named James. He told him that he was going to sponsor a refugee, a fifteen-year-old girl from Austria. He was referring to my sister. He read the details of my sister's identity to James and then asked him to please notify him when my sister's papers had been approved by the immigration authorities. Then he asked me, "Where do I reach you when I am notified that your sister's immigration has been approved?" I hesitated. I didn't know if I should tell him that I was staying with the Abramsons. But I decided to trust him – sort of the silent agreement of thieves under cover. I told him some distant relatives were trying to get me sent back, so I didn't want them to find out where I lived.

He said, "Tell me, who are these distant relatives of yours? " I told him of Dr. Freeder and Mrs. Hausenball and he said, "I know who they are – Dr. Freeder is an S.O.B and Mrs. Hausenball is a roaring bitch."

I agreed with all my heart. Heading then placed another call to someone and he said, "I am sitting here with a refugee boy. He has relatives here who want to send him back through the Woburn House. This is a terrible disgrace and I am going to tell them so."

*　　*　　*　　*

Martha Klein shares some poignant facts that don't seem to appear in any biographical summaries of her late husband's remarkable life story. "When Ed turned sixteen in England he did not exactly get a visa," she explains. "He was rounded up with others who had escaped, and as the British government was not sure if they were enemies or refugees, they just sent all these people to either Australia or Canada, and put them in internment camps – the way we put Japanese in camps during the war. Ed was in one of these camps two or three years, until the war was over. At that point, someone in Canada sponsored him and thus allowed him to stay in Canada. He was supposed to go to Australia but for some reason did not get on that boat, and that was very fortunate, as that boat was sunk. His next option – our luck – was Canada. After relegated to an internment camp there for three years, he enrolled in the University of Toronto and did so well that he survived the whole eight years on scholarships."

Mrs. Klein adds with good humor that Edmund was a little older than some of his fellow students when he started college. "He was already in his 30s when I met him (while they were both perusing books in a drug store near Harvard University). He was ten years older than I. My parents had a fit!"

*　　*　　*　　*　　*

One could make the argument that Dr. Edmund Klein, like Salvador Dali, understood how to court the news media. Both knew how to garner headlines, in part through their respective areas of genius, in part through a penchant for at least some controversy. Klein's important medical research, and his opinions and views, mattered greatly – and mainstream media took note. *Newsweek* magazine, in its July 14, 1982 issue, published an article titled "Suntans and Skin Cancer," and featured Dr. Klein's comments extensively. He was quoted as explaining that ultra-violet rays lead to atrophy of the skin and that exposure to sunlight has a cumulative effect. In other words, *Newsweek* wrote, "risk of cancer doesn't go back to zero with the fading of each summer's tan. It increases year after year. 'The clock is ticking,' says Klein, 'from your first exposure to the sun.'" (Newsweek, July 14, 1982, p. 85).

Remarkably, the national Sunday newspaper magazine supplement, *Parade*, on September 11, 1977, featured a photo of Dr. Klein under the headline, The Men Who Spend Your Money To Keep You Healthy, and noted in the caption: "Edmund Klein of Buffalo, who found cure for skin cancer, in front of centrifuge...." One has rarely if ever seen "cancer" and "cure" together in a definitive, conclusive statement of such medical and historical importance.

Dr. Klein even made it into the iconic *Ask Ann Landers* column. Headlined "Dr. Klein Debunks Hair Dye Scare," published in *The Buffalo News* (date unknown), the column featured a reader who worried about allegations that hair dye might cause cancer. Landers' response, in part, went as follows: "Dr. Edmund Klein, a most distinguished and world-renowned skin cancer specialist at the Roswell Park Memorial Institute, New York's state Center for Treatment, Control and Research of Cancer, had this to say: 'Many of my patients, including those who have a tendency to develop skin cancers, as well as those who have already developed skin cancers, have been dyeing their hair for decades. To the best of my knowledge, not one cancer has occurred in these patients that could be traced to hair dyes....'"

Rather amusingly, Dr. Klein appeared yet again in Ann Landers' popular nationally syndicated column, in a piece called "Just

Ask Dr. Klein." It seems a 22-year-old male wrote to Landers, complaining about sweaty palms, noting he didn't sweat excessively anywhere else "but when I find myself in certain social situations my hands sometimes drip. This can be pretty darned embarrassing." He signed himself, A KISS INSTEAD OF A HANDSHAKE, IN WASHINGTON, D.C.

The columnist's advice was for the lad to check out page 861 of "The Ann Landers Encyclopedia," where he would find a piece on "Clammy Hands" by Dr. Edmund Klein, "a superb dermatologist in Buffalo, N.Y. He says, 'In severe cases, carry absorbent materials, such as tissue paper that has been pretreated with aluminum chloride.' He says a lot more, of course, so I hope you'll go to the library and look it up."

Dr. Klein, whose photo made the pages of *LIFE* magazine during his active days as a researcher, appeared in this *New York Times* headline on Friday, July 30, 1999 – his obituary: "Edmund Klein, 77, an Expert on

Skin Cancer – Praise for cancer work, controversy for a remark":

Dr. Edmund Klein, whose pioneering work on skin cancer was honored with a Clinical Research Award from the Albert and Mary Lasker Foundation in 1972, died on Saturday at Millard Fillmore Hospital in Buffalo. He was 77 and lived in Williamsville, N.Y., a Buffalo suburb.

The causes were complications of diabetes and congestive heart failure, his family said.

One of Dr. Klein's early insights, that skin cancer could be treated externally, led him to cancer research in dermatology...He also advanced the use of immunotherapy, in which the body's own defenses are alerted to fend off tumors. This involved the application of agents to stimulate the immune system and pointed the way toward the use of interferon and interleukins in today's cancer therapy....

The Times obituary, written by Wolfgang Saxon, also reported the controversy Dr.

Klein created when, in an interview with a *Reader's Digest* journalist, the doctor stated "authoritatively" that President Lyndon B. Johnson had been treated for skin cancer. The *Times* obituary went on to say that the Johnson family and White House doctors "denied the report of skin cancer, although the removal of less serious spots from the President's skin was confirmed by his personal physician. Dr. Klein said he had based his remark on a phone call he had received from the Johnson White House, which, he said, had made a general inquiry about a possible treatment for skin cancer. He said he had been authorized to diagnose the condition by a Johnson family representative, whom he declined to identify."

Martha Klein told me that her late husband included several other luminaries among his patient base, including Stavros Niarchos, the multi-billionaire Greek shipping tycoon; the zany comic actor Zero Mostell; legendary movie star John Wayne; and a very popular American female singer who's still living and thus cannot be named.

And then there was a certain Spanish artist.

"Salvador Dali calling for Dr. Klein. I was very thrilled with that call," Martha Klein told me. She had no idea of the adventure that lay ahead.

CHAPTER 2

Drawings Supplant Payment for Medical Treatments

Dali and Dr. Klein met for the first time at the St. Regis Hotel in New York City. The stately hotel on 5th Avenue and 55th Street was Dali and Madame Dali's winter home away from home for many years, roughly from December to April. Wintering in New York meant lots of commissions for the artist, including some remarkable and at times controversial society portraits.

Details of their many meetings together – usually over long dinners, not only in New York but also in Paris and Port Lligat, Spain – are unavailable. Martha Klein reminds us that her husband's work was highly confidential, for obvious reasons. He never really discussed any details with her or anyone else, taking patient confidentiality very seriously indeed. In fact, we know of no photographs of Klein and Dali together, though there was certainly no injunction against it. One might presume that Dali was probably insistent about not publicizing in any way his one-on-one sessions with Dr. Klein, whom he called his "guardian angel," a moniker that appeared on most of the drawings he created for Klein. It would simply have been out of character and counterintuitive for the flamboyant Dali – who put himself out there so publicly and proudly – to reveal in any way a disconcerting health condition. Likewise, Dr. Klein – not a stranger to a certain eccentricity of his own – was nevertheless a rigorous defender of doctor/patient confidentiality.

(I know of only one reference to Dr. Klein in a Dali book. It appears in Dali secretary Enrique Sabater's 1998 book, "A Sabater Con Un Abrazon En El Quin Elisabet": "Other doctors also have Dali's esteem and confidence. Doctor Carballeira, his usual doctor when in New York; Doctor Trueta, whom we used to visit in the evenings in his house at Santa Cristina d'Aro; Severo Ochoa (the Noble Prize winner, often accompanied by Doctor Oro) who came on friendly visits to the Saint-Regis in New York; Doctor Francisco Dalmau from Palamos; he looked after him by phone for many months; the daily consultation took place at an exact time, three o'clock in the morning Spanish time; Doctor Jose Sarro in Barcelona, Doctor

Vidal Teixidor; Doctor Klein in Buffalo (USA) and so on."
(p. 69-71).

We do know, though, that Dr. Klein administered some form of treatment to Dali during their meetings. But no payment was asked for; Edmund simply wanted Salvador to get better. In return for such selflessness, the Surrealist master would bring either a Dali book or a sketchpad to their private meetings and create a drawing – often some form of an angelic motif – and dedicate it, "Pour mon ange ("For my angel"), Doctor Klein." (Although Dali was Spanish, he often wrote in French.)

Their rendezvous spanned nearly a decade, and the resultant 15 drawings Dali made for his friend and physician date from 1973 to 1980. The predominant theme is angels, for that is what Dr. Klein was to Salvador Dali – his "guardian angel" and a real testament to the extremely high regard in which Dali held Klein. In fact, on one drawing with angel imagery, Dali actually wrote, "Guardian Angel No. II, First = Gala." Dox Quixote was another theme seen in some of the Klein collection, emblematic of the indomitable character after which Dali fancied himself and his friend, Edmund Klein.

Amy Szymoniak, one of the Klein's' daughters, remembers the time the entire family traveled to Paris and actually was extended the extraordinary opportunity to stay in Dali's luxurious suite at the historic Hotel Meurice, while Dali was away. Amy, just 14 years old at the time, kept a hand-written diary of their adventure, which also included time in Italy and even an Audience with the Pope. In her diary entry for Oct. 15, 1977, the young teen matter-of-factly wrote, "We are in Paris...we are staying in the suite of Salvador Dali. It has a living room with marble floors, two bedrooms with balconies from which you can see the Eiffel Tower and Arch of Triumph in one glance."

Amy, now an attorney, wasn't the only Klein family member with recollections of how the Dali/Klein friendship left an impression on them. Dr. Lawrence Klein, MD, a dermatologist and dermatopathologist at the University of South Carolina – who in later years became host and associate producer of The Bluegrass Sound on the South Carolina ETV Radio Network – recalls a meeting with Dali himself:

"It was a very brief meeting. I don't remember the year, but it may have been the summer I worked at Sloan Kettering and lived up about 72nd Street and York Avenue on the Upper East Side. Either that or a few years later when I was in New York for something. It most likely would have been the early to mid-1970s, as I recall. My father called and said if I could get to the United Nations apartment building in an hour or so, I would be able to meet Salvador Dali.

"It probably would have been Mary Lasker's apartment suite at UN Plaza, downstairs from Ethel Kennedy, as I recall. She had a spiral staircase and original Picassos, Cezanne's and Chagall's on the wall – even in the bathroom. Again, to the best of my recollection," the younger Dr. Klein reminisced. "When I got there and briefly met Dali, he was also wearing a suit, but it was a gray pinstripe suit with the stripes on the pants going opposite in direction to the stripes on the jacket. I'd have guessed it was personally designed.

"He did have the famous moustache, and said something along the lines of, 'I love this man,' (referring to Edmund Klein) or words to that effect, and maybe something like "he is my good ami..." That's all I remember, except that something made me think at the time, and reconfirmed in looking at his artistic works, especially where I knew sort of what he was doing (like 'Don Quixote Genetique')* that he was actually more genius than lunatic and that I only had a mere snippet of ability to understand his level of thinking, or ability to express himself artistically."

(* The reference here is to one of the drawings Dali did for Edmund Klein, on which he added, as part of his dedicatory comments, "Don Quixote genetique." This is explained in further detail in Chapter 6.)

CHAPTER 3

Treasure in a Buffalo Bank Vault

From the early 1970s to 1980, Dr. Edmund Klein enjoyed a host of private meetings with Salvador Dali, in New York, France, and Spain. These occasions melded direct treatments with great food and what surely must have been captivating conversation. *Toronto Star* writer Isabel Teotonio, in an August 3, 2009 story, wrote that Dali and Dr. Klein's private medical appointments "were often followed by dinners and late-night discussions about philosophy, science and religion."

At every private session, Dali did a sketch for his guardian angel, inscribing each one, dating all but one, and signing all but one. In the end, a unique and remarkable collection emerged, featuring horses and riders, Don Quixote figures (including one with sidekick Sancho Panza), angels in various forms, a

DNA double-helix drawing in black crayon, and an embracing couple watching a shooting star.

It appears Dr. Klein was actually more intrigued with Dali's intellect — especially his ability to be impressively conversant in things scientific — than with his art. It's not that he didn't respect Dali's creations, his widow assures, but rather that his interest simply lay less in Dali's art than in his genius mind and engaging personality.

From every indication, the renowned dermatologist's ministrations to Dali were successful. After the last drawing gifted to Klein, dated 1980 and executed while the artist's health was steadily declining, Dali lived another nine years, finally succumbing to heart failure at age 84 on January 23, 1989. Dr. Klein passed on July 24, 1999, at age 77, due to complications from diabetes mellitus and congestive heart failure.

What survived — in addition to great memories and experiences on the part of the Klein family, and a legacy of revolutionary cancer research – was a very special collection of Dali drawings, prints and sculpture. Unsure of just what to do with so extensive a collection of specialized original and obviously valuable pieces of handiwork – by arguably the most famous artist in the world – Martha Klein decided to store them in safe deposit boxes. Unknown to anyone except her, the Klein children, and a few friends, the artwork remained sequestered in a downtown Buffalo bank vault for more than three decades.

Then, in April of 2008, a newspaper article in *The Buffalo News* (Buffalo, New York), set in motion what would become the Klein-Dali collection's resurrection from its many years in darkness and obscurity. For students of public relations, it was a lesson in the potentially powerful impact a single press release can have. It was a few weeks earlier that I was named a columnist (blogger) for The Salvador Dali Society, Inc., of Redondo Beach, California. I had issued a press release about this appointment to *The Buffalo News*, expecting they might publish a one- or two-liner, since the national Dali Society now had a local angle.

To my surprise, a reporter from the newspaper, Louise Continelli, called to say she thought my work with Dali sounded interesting and that she wanted to do a profile of me, to be accompanied by my photo holding a Dali book. An excellent story and picture ran on April 13, 2008 – proving the clout of a press release and the power of the press.

A few days later, I received a phone call from Martha Klein. She explained that she owned a rather special collection of original Salvador Dali sketches and related works, giving me a concise version of the incredible backstory. Would I be interested, she asked, in accompanying her and her two daughters (they both reside in Western New York, while the Klein sons – both doctors – live out of state) on a visit to the downtown bank vault that housed the Dali's. My answer, of course, was a resounding yes.

What a thrill it was to go take in these unbelievable treasures! One by one, I went through them carefully, cautioning this wonderfully gracious and fortunate family to handle each piece as if it were the Hope Diamond. The many years of their being in total darkness paid dividends; condition is key when it comes to artworks, and these sketches and the book pages or sketchpads on which they were drawn were in pristine condition. I was taken by their beauty.

Mrs. Klein – a benevolent and savvy matriarchal figure in charge of the collection now – revealed that it was time to take it out of storage and sell the works one by one. She knew they had significant value, and that monies made from their sale would be put to good use. I was deeply honored when she asked me to become consultant to her collection, involving its cataloging, exhibition, and marketing. It was time to get to work.

CHAPTER 4

Making Headlines Worldwide

The first action item was to get the Klein Collection cataloged. What a surreal experience when our photographer set up a make-shift photo studio in a room off the main floor in the basement of HSBC Bank in downtown Buffalo, just outside the massive steel doors of the vault. A bank security guard kept a watchful eye on us throughout several long sessions, as we went about our rather unorthodox business of shooting pictures of original Salvador Dali drawings finally liberated from their pitch black safe deposit boxes and thrust into the bright lights of the photo shoot.

The published 30-page catalog came out beautifully.

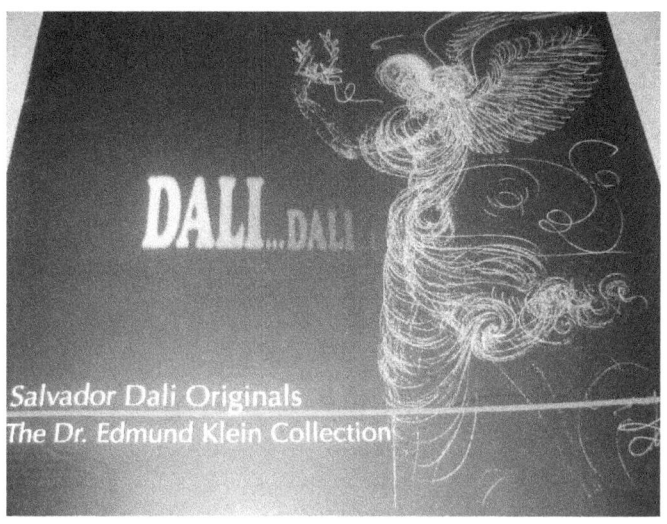

Titled "Salvador Dali Originals: The Dr. Edmund Klein Collection," its cover (photo by Glenn Pazian) featured an image of what came to be known among us as the "Cover Angel." It was easily the most exquisite drawing in the collection, executed on two blank pages of Dali's stunning cookbook, "Les Diners de Gala." I'll never forget a comment made some years later by renowned American artist Harvey Breverman when he saw the work for the first time in the exhibition we arranged of the Klein collection: "Because it was in ink and in a book," Breverman observed, "there was no room for error. Making a mistake was not an option. The drawing was executed flawlessly." *(An excerpt of Breverman's written thoughts about the Klein drawings appears later in this book.)*

I had the pleasure of authoring the text of the catalog, which began this way: "This is the story of two great twentieth century pioneers who came together in a remarkable union of medical and artistic genius: Dr. Edmund Klein and painter Salvador Dali. It resulted in a unique collection of original drawings that, until the publication of this catalog, have never before been seen by the art world."

Martha Klein and I were getting her Dali collection ready for its debut, and as a major first step, the catalog was a success. It turned out so well. Now it was time to determine if the media would see the news value of what we had. We contacted our hometown newspaper, *The Buffalo News*, and they instantly smelled a fabulous story. Veteran reporter Dale Anderson, in an article headlined "Stored Salvador Dali sketches emerge" and sub-titled, "Drawings depict physician as artist's guardian angel," wrote:

Sketches by surrealist artist Salvador Dali, given by Dali to a Buffalo physician and held in safe deposit boxes for more than 30 years, are about to see the light of day.

The family of the late Dr. Edmund Klein, who was chief of dermatology at Roswell Park Cancer Institute and a renowned cancer researcher, recently decided to offer the group of 15 original drawings and a statue for sale. Their existence was announced Thursday in a story on an art news Web site, www.artdaily.org.

"Frankly, the family never knew what to do with [the collection]," said Paul Chimera, a Dali specialist from Amherst and author of the artdaily.org story. "But they knew they were valuable, so they kept them in safekeeping."

Chimera wrote that Dali first called Klein in 1972, the year that Klein received the prestigious Albert Lasker Award, and they

met numerous times at the St. Regis Hotel in Manhattan, where Dali stayed during the winter months, and in his home in Spain. Dali died in 1989. Klein died 10 years later.

"Dali considered Dr. Klein his guardian angel," Chimera said. "I think Dr. Klein probably treated Dali for a form of skin cancer."

The guardian angel theme runs through the sketches, executed on sketch pads and on blank pages in books, Chimera noted. The statue, he added, is a silver figure of John the Baptist cast from a mold fashioned by Dali himself.
The most notable angel, reproduced on artdaily.org, is inscribed in the frontispiece of "The Dinners of Gala," a book of Dali lithographs.

Chimera, who is advising the Klein family on the sale, said that contacts are being made with prospective buyers to purchase the entire collection. Chimera estimated that the collection was worth "six figures,"

and that the angel sketch in "The Dinners of Gala" was worth at least $75,000 by itself." (*The Buffalo News*, Friday, Aug. 8, 2008).

Artdaily.org headlined its story "Secret Salvador Dali Drawings Discovered; Personal Physician Revealed to be Artist's Angel." News of the "hidden" Dali treasure spread like proverbial wild fire. It came as no surprise that the Associated Press picked up the story, but Mrs. Klein and I were astounded at how rapidly the story spread world-wide. Our phones were ringing off the wall and in our pockets. Several local TV stations in Buffalo broadcast reports on the collection, interviewing the photogenic Martha Klein and her daughters, Amy and Rene. I appeared as well, in one case with Martha live on a 6 a.m. Buffalo television show that featured "unusual things" going on in the city.

News of the "secret" Dali drawings appeared in *The New York Times, USA Today, The Boston Globe, San Francisco Examiner, New York Daily News, Miami*

Herald, *Washington Post*, Forbes magazine, and literally hundreds of other newspapers and online news sites around the world – in countries such as England, Spain, France, Canada, Taiwan, Singapore, Japan, Israel, and Australia, among many others.

The *Toronto Star* of Ontario, Canada, sent a reporter down to interview Martha Klein and daughter Amy, and the *Expresso* newspaper from Portugal dispatched journalist Ricardo Lourenco to Buffalo to tell its readers about the hidden Dali stash suddenly revealed after all these years.

Now it was time to show the public the sketches in the flesh.

CHAPTER 5

Collection Makes Its Public Debut

Martha Klein and I arranged to exhibit her collection for the first time ever, at the U.B. Anderson Gallery on the campus of The State University of New York at Buffalo. The university was thrilled with the idea from the start and was extremely enthusiastic and helpful in coordinating the myriad details that go into an undertaking such as this.

Also thrilled were editors at *The Buffalo News*, who demonstrated the news value of the Klein collection's first showing with a dramatic front-page story, including a color photograph of Martha Klein and her daughter Amy with some of the artwork, in a story titled "Dali gifts going public at last." News staff reporter Tom Buckham, who came out to Martha's daughter Rene's home to see the works and interview the family and me, wrote the following page-one article:

A darkened bank vault is no place for Salvador Dali's exuberant, surreal art.

So art lovers were happy last August when 15 sketches by the celebrated Spanish artist were brought to light by the widow of Dr. Edmund Klein after they had been locked away in downtown safe deposit boxes for more than 30 years.

But they've remained out of the public eye.

Now, after framing at Benjaman's Art Gallery on Elmwood Avenue, the drawings are being readied for their first showing from next Saturday to Aug. 27 in the University at Buffalo's Anderson Gallery, along with four other Dali works owned by Martha Klein – two lithographs, a watercolor (sic) and a silver statuette.

All were given to her late husband, a renowned Buffalo dermatologist, in return for his treatment of Dali's skin cancer over nearly a decade, starting in 1972.

Klein, whose patients also included actors John Wayne and Zero Mostel, got along famously with the highly imaginative artist and hesitated to bill him for the visits to his winter residence in a New York City hotel or home in France and Spain.

So Dali "gave him a drawing each time," Martha Klein recalled...as a team from UB Galleries boxed the collection for the trip to Anderson Gallery on Martha Jackson Place in University Heights.

The largest pieces – lithographs and watercolor (sic), also gifts from the artist – were hung in the Kleins' home, but there was no room for the drawings, so they went into deposit boxes for safekeeping.

Avoiding exposure to sunlight in a temperature-controlled room for all those years wasn't the worst fate for the delicate drawings – including several angels – executed in Dali books, sketch pads and a photography catalog and dedicated to "mon ami Klein" or "mon Angel le Doctor Klein," said Paul Chimera, a Dali specialist from Amherst and the family's consultant on the collection.

On balance, the vault is "probably a pretty good place for them," Chimera said.

The Klein collection will be exhibited with two Dali paintings owned by UB and four from Niagara University's Castellani Art Museum.

Martha Klein, whose husband died 10 years ago, a decade after Dali, hopes the exhibition will attract a buyer or buyers. Though the family's collection has not been appraised, she is confident it would fetch at least enough to pay for the education of her nine grandchildren.

She would prefer to sell the set intact, she said, because breaking it up "would spoil the story."

A pretty lady out on the town needs appropriate attire, of course. No expense was spared in dressing up the sketches in lavish frames, custom-fashioned by

Benjaman's Gallery of Buffalo, New York. It was an unusual and somewhat tricky affair, because we insisted on maintaining the integrity of the drawings as they were originally executed – whether in books, on sketchpads, on an exhibition catalog and, in one case, on the back of a technical paper Dr. Klein had co-authored. Consequently the hefty books themselves were framed, and that required some custom-framing agility the gallery handled with aplomb.

The first ever exhibition of the Klein Dali drawings was a big hit. Also on display at this once-in-a-lifetime exhibit were several graphic works lent from the Castellani Art Museum on the campus of Niagara University, north of Buffalo. And the two stunning Dali originals owned by the State University of New York at Buffalo: "Portrait of Katherine Cornell" (1951) and "Labyrinth" (1941). For those who couldn't attend the exhibition, we created a website (www.drkleindalicollection.blogspot.com), which featured a link to a panoramic slide show of all the works. (That slide show is no longer operational, for reasons unknown.)

The exhibition, we would learn, was one of the best-attended exhibitions ever at the gallery. Sandra H. Olsen, Ph.D., Director, UB Art Galleries, wrote in a letter to Martha Klein in August of 2009: "Thank you for the generous loan to UB Anderson Gallery of the beautiful drawings by Salvador Dali in your collection. The exhibition was wonderful and it was enjoyed by so many! I can write with all honesty that an exhibition or event at UB Anderson Gallery will never again receive such incredible international attention from the press. Only such a compelling narrative about the friendship that developed between two geniuses in science and art and the opportunity for the public to see drawings by Dali that were previously never exhibited, could attract such attention and capture the interest of such a broad and diverse audience."

One visitor to the show was Buffalo-based artist Harvey Breverman, whose paintings and prints appear in major museums around the globe. Deeply impressed by the Klein collection, Breverman, on July 26, 2009, wrote a personal review of the UB

Anderson Gallery exhibition of the Klein Collection, titled, "Dali as Draughtsman: Where Dreams and Reality Merge":

The extraordinary variety of drawings in the Dr. Edmund Klein Family Collection commemorates a mutual bond of trust, respect and admiration between an artist and his physician, both world-renowned in their respective achievements.

Simultaneously, these superb dedicatory drawings gifted to Dr. Klein in person spanning nearly a decade in the 1970s are profoundly poignant, precisely because they convey aesthetically and poetically an intermingling of art and science, symbol and text.

In the grand tradition of "livres d'artistes" (artists' illustrated books whose frontispiece may include a personal note to collaborators – publisher, printer, writer or poet), Dali's dramatically embellished pictorial gestures are testimonials to "remembrance." Drawn on eight double-page spreads in Dr. Klein's presence at

various sites, Dali fixes on a moment in time that identifies the circumstance but not its details.

I stood silently in the presence of the Klein drawings, scrutinizing and revisiting each idiomatic shift, making comparisons, reflecting and reconsidering. I tracked their marks that crayon or litho pencil makes on textured paper and followed the trajectory of a fine pen point as its linear density criss-crossed an image, emphasizing this passage or that.

Dali's text and signatures are integral parts of the larger drama. An artist's last name, if short enough (Miro, Klee, Picasso, Klimt et al), can become a potent pictorial and calligraphic symbol within the body of the work.

Hybridization abounds. In one drawing, Dali's signature serves as a pictorial armature (pedestal) for the text it balances above. In another, the top of a diagonal bar of the letter D (Dali) forms a cross as it integrates and contextualizes meaning.

Likewise, the descender of the letter K
(Klein) flows into and becomes the arm of
a figure pulling a horse.

In a swirl of concentric oval or with incisive
linear tracery both calligraphic yet
descriptive, Dali articulates the topography
and the bay at Port Lligat. Stretching the
métier, Dali's "certificate of authenticity
for a small sculpture" is a dramatic tour de
force that utilizes brush, quill or reed pen.

And in a single breath, Dali conceals and
reveals in notations, jottings and drawings,
a visionary world filled with cryptic,
ambiguous and unpredictable
iconography.

CHAPTER 6

Notes to a Guardian Angel

Dali himself offered some insights into the meaning of some of the drawings. And two members of the Klein family – attorney Amy Szymoniak and dermatologist Dr. Peter Klein – have either memories of what their father had told them about some of the works, or their own special observations and insights.

The first work reproduced in the Catalog of the collection (whose hand-written inscription by Dali has never quite been deciphered), came to be known as simply "Dermatology." Amy recalls it being explained to her father by Dali that the steed's rider was supposed to represent Dali, while the man guiding its direction is meant to be Dr. Klein, just as Dr. Klein led Dali in the right direction with respect to his medical issues.

One of the strongest images in the collection was the crayon drawing that came to be known as "Dali & DNA." It depicted the double-helix molecular structure of DNA. Amy Szymoniak notes, "I shall never forget my father's rendition of his conversation with Dali, as Dali had his sketchbook and pen in hand. They were discussing the philosophical aspects of the merging between medicine and religion. Out of this discussion came Dali's version of Jacob's ladder, comprised of DNA molecules intertwined with the angels ascending to Heaven. The second angel represents my father with the medical staff in hand."

The drawing of a kneeling angel holding an olive branch, drawn on a catalog from the long-defunct Sidney Janis Gallery in New York (1976), featured an eye-opening inscription by Dali. Interestingly enough, the dedication to Klein finds that Dali misspelled his physician friend's name – unwittingly transposing the "e" and the "l"! But on this work Dali actually noted that Dr. Klein was second only to Dali's beloved wife, Gala, as his guardian angel.

The biggest and boldest work in the Dr.
Klein Dali Collection was drawn in what
came to be known as the "Candy Box" book
(Dali, Abrams, 1968), because its striking
gold dust jacket, designed by Dali (for which
he won a European book cover design
award) was inspired after Dali
contemplated the gold foil in a box of
chocolates. The drawing shows the popular
"spinning man" figure that Dali was fond of
drawing, holding a lance and shield like a
troubadour or Don Quixote-like figure.
Indeed, Dali wrote "Don Quixote
genetique" as part of the inscription –
melding the Don Quixote imagery with a
nod to genetics, acknowledging the science-
minded Edmund Klein.

But the famed dermatologist's son, Dr.
Peter Klein, who does medical research
today at the University of Pennsylvania,
offered another perspective that may
forever change the way we look at this so-
called spinning man draftsmanship from
Dali. The younger Klein astutely pointed out
that the morphology of a human
chromosome looks almost identical to the

zig-zag line style of Dali's spinning man figures (see diagram). He believes there is little question that Dali was aware of this when he created these images.

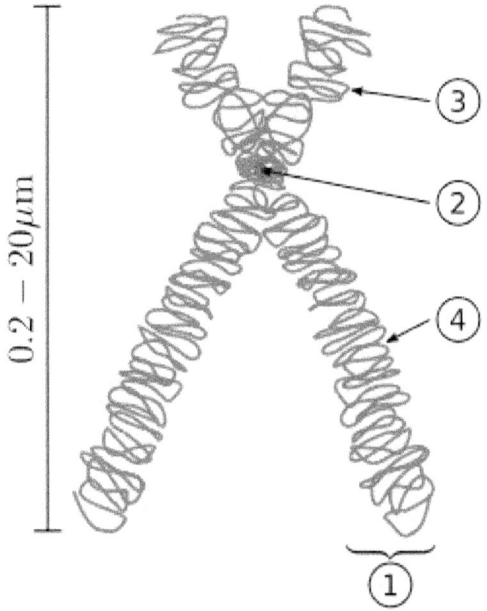

The graceful angel drawn in the book, "Les Diners de Gala," is undisputed as the finest drawing in the collection. Its delicate line is exquisite. It is significant to note the striking similarity between this work and one called "Gradiva," an ink drawing published in Dali's autobiography, "The Secret Life of Salvador Dali." The centerpiece of the collection, it is now in the hands of a Venezuelan doctor, last we knew.

The gallant Don Quixote figure astride a horse, executed in black crayon on the frontispiece of the book, "Dali by Dali," was blown up in a far larger reproduction, framed, and displayed in the patient waiting room of Dr. Klein's dermatology office in Williamsville, New York.

Sometimes it was Dali's signature and how it accorded with other elements in a work that commanded special attention. Of an angel drawing showing a frolicking angelic figure with a star positioned at her fingertip, Dr. Klein's daughter Amy noted, "Perhaps the most telling of Dali's and my father's friendship is found in the dedication of this 1979 sketch, wherein Dali interconnected both of their names. The intertwining of their names exemplified not only Dali's fascination with the merging of science and religion, but also the fusion of an unbreakable friendship and a molecular-like melding of two great minds. Similar to the Dali & DNA drawing, the dedication utilizes a series of straight lines with connecting dots."

What we came to call the "Double Drawing" featured, on the left side of a two-page spread from the book, "The World of Salvador Dali," the image of both a standing Don Quixote and his sidekick, Sancho Panza riding a mule. On the adjoining page, Dali drew a kneeling angel figure holding an olive branch. Remarkably, the 1980 work features four signatures by Dali.

Then there was the work dubbed "Triple Drawing" – a declared favorite of the Kleins' daughter, Amy – featuring a pair of lovers gazing upon a shooting star; a standing Don Quixote figure; and a Don Quixote figure on horseback.

The final work presented in the Catalog – "Don Quixote on horseback" – tells something of a sad story. By 1980, Salvador Dali was growing increasingly debilitated by a confluence of physical and psychological factors. His declining health was evident in the quality of line in this drawing, made on a sketchpad. It appears that, in the date Dali put on the drawing, he initially wrote "1979" but then altered the "7" to become an "8." He then dated it a second time, to the right, "1980." While the hindquarters of the horse were drawn nicely, the horse's head and legs suggest a weakened hand of the ailing master draftsman. In fact, the horse's face has a hauntingly vacant look, as if to foretell that Dali knew his own life was coming to an end.

CHAPTER 7

Ignoring Detractors and Taking the High Road

As with just about every story, every adventure, every remarkable journey, there are invariably occasional dark clouds to intrude upon otherwise clear and sunny days. We experienced our share of stormy weather along the way. We're not going to mention names. But it seems it's true: when you're at the top, there will always be people determined to knock you down.

Of particular note was a reputed member of a Dali "research group" of some sort, allegedly based in New York, who insisted that we needed to procure a Descharnes certificate of authenticity (COA) on all the Klein works – a prospect that would have cost what Mrs. Klein and I thought an inordinate (and unnecessary) sum. Without that COA, the source said, the collection might be determined by this group to be "not right."

Never mind that the collection's provenance was second to none. That news of the collection made international headlines from New York to New Zealand. Or that the curator of the Salvador Dali Museum itself, in St. Petersburg, Florida – home of the world's largest collection of Dali originals – wrote in a September 12, 2006 letter to the Kleins' daughter, Amy Szymoniak, "What a fascinating story regarding your father and Dali...These wonderful dedicated sketches and drawings in books that Dali did for your father over the years are more valuable together than separated. In several drawings you can see that Dali took time to render the images with detail and thought regarding the recipient. They also portray the familiar images associated with Dali, such as the spinning man and the angel, along with his fascination for new scientific discoveries in the DNA drawing."

Moreover, the Klein Collection was authenticated by Bernard Ewell, a well-known senior appraiser and author, specializing in Salvador Dali, and who three times was commissioned to appraise the multi-million-dollar collection of the Florida Dali Museum. Ewell has probably testified in art fraud cases more often than any other expert witness.

Indications of jealousy wore many faces. A for-instance was on the occasion of the collection's sales exhibition, titled "Dali's Angels," at Benjaman's Gallery in Buffalo. Martha Klein recalls a pretentious woman – "she was obviously jealous!" – who had approached her like a fussy schoolmarm to rebuke, "It's pronounced 'Dah-LEE,' not 'Dolly!'" Unfazed, the classy Mrs. Klein graciously took the high road and simply thanked the woman for attending the November 5, 2010 reception.

In another case, Martha sent me on an overnight trip to Staten Island, New York, along with four or five of the sketches. A California art dealer specializing in Dali had agreed to meet me there to look at the Dali's for possible purchase. He was instantly blown away by them, he said, and claimed he already had a buyer for the entire collection. None of it turned out to be true.

Over the years, we also saw pathetic forgeries of the Klein sketches popping up on ebay. One even found itself in an auction in Spain, until we spotted it in the auction's catalog and Mrs. Klein immediately wrote a terse but pointed e-mail to the auctioneers, who promptly yanked the bogus work from the sale. And there was the time we put much of the collection on exhibition in a gallery in SoHo in New York, only to witness the gallery go belly-up a few months later.

Undeterred by such roadblocks – some of them put in our path intentionally, others just the result of how business sometimes goes – the Dr. Edmund Klein Collection, piece by piece, eventually was sold. The whole process spanned about eight years.

Two works went to a young attorney on the Island of Malta. One drawing was purchased by an attorney in Mexico City. The beautiful "cover angel" was acquired by a physician in Venezuela. Another work is now in the collection of an American television producer.

Throughout our journey, Martha Klein and I learned to ignore the naysayers and stay focused on the positive. We understood that dedicatory drawings would be more difficult to sell, given their personalized nature. It was a test of patience and perseverance for us both. More importantly, it was a commitment to taking the high road and staying positive and honest in the face of an art market riddled with so many unsavory, dishonest and unscrupulous characters, scoundrels, and crooks. In the end, to channel a well-known Sinatra song, we did it our way.

For me personally, it created a lasting friendship with Martha Klein and her lovely family. Martha is one of the kindest, most savvy and generous people I have ever known. And very humble. She never once let her good fortune get in the way of her down-to-earth nature. Indeed, it was I who occasionally felt the need to remind her of just how amazing it was that she had this connection with two giants in the worlds of art and medicine.

The Klein family collection inevitably reminds us of just six other family collections in the world that involved this kind of Dali exclusivity: the Argillet collection of Paris, France; the Albaretto collection of Turin, Italy; the Moore collection of Cadaques, Spain; the Descharnes collection of Paris; the Sabater collection of Andorra; and the Morse collection, originally of Cleveland, Ohio and then of St. Petersburg, Florida. The late A. Reynolds and Eleanor R. Morse amassed the largest collection in the world of Dali paintings (and works in other mediums) and became benefactors of the Salvador Dali Museum in St. Petersburg.

For this author, serving as adviser to the Dr. Klein Dali Collection was more than and honor and privilege. It was an opportunity to forge a great friendship with a great family. And while I met and spent several hours with Salvador Dali in 1973 and 1974 in New York – unquestionably the most memorable experience of my life – I actually did have the pleasure of meeting Dr. Klein as well.

Regrettably, it was a short-lived occasion. I had arranged to meet him at his dermatology office on a Saturday, as I recall, for the expressed purpose of interviewing him for an article I planned to write for a Dali publication of which I was editor at the time. But when I showed up and introduced myself, the doctor was seriously under the weather. He apologized in finding it necessary to call off the interview, pledging to reschedule. It never happened. Sadly, his health continued its downward spiral and I never did get my story. Well, except for the one you've just read.

I regret that Dr. Klein and I never got our chance to become friends. Not only was he a titan in his professional life, but it was clear he was an engaging, colorful personality and a genuinely kind soul. A glimpse into his more human side was afforded in a July 28, 1999 article, shortly after his death, published in the *Philadelphia Daily News*. Writer/editor Yvette Ousley noted, "Often delayed because of the time he took with each patient, Klein was revered for his profound love of humanity and the warmth he always shared. His clinical acumen and determination in tackling seemingly hopeless cases often encouraged referrals from around the world. "He lives life very fully," said his son, Dr. Peter Klein...an assistant professor of medicine at the University of Pennsylvania School of medicine. "He was full of warmth and had this profound appreciation for humanity that mixed with his clinical research. His patients just loved him."

Extraordinary insight into both the personal and professional side of Edmund Klein can be found in the book, "The Miracle Finders." Under the eye-opening heading, **"Klein Finds a Cure for Skin Cancer,"** author Donald Robinson wrote, "The first time I saw Dr. Klein was on that winter evening in New York City as he lectured on his skin cancer work to a group of distinguished researchers at Sloan Kettering. He showed a long series of before-and-after pictures of men and women with mutilated, cancerous faces and bodies who had been completely cured. The Sloan Kettering men were very impressed. Afterward, I talked with him for hours in an empty conference room at Sloan Kettering.

"He proved to be a delightfully informal, effusive chap, full of good humor, warmth, and wisecracks in English and Yiddish. He was born in Vienna in 1921, the son of a very poor rabbi. 'How did you happen to get interested in being a doctor?
I inquired.

"'I didn't want to be a rabbi.'

"'To escape theology, you went into medicine?'

"'Well, not necessarily. I don't think you can practice medicine without practicing theology.'...

"'Didn't you want to be rich?'

"'Sure, I wanted to be rich, but I thought there were other things that were more important.'

"'Such as?'

"'Such as doing things for people.'"

Martha Klein recalls an incident, while she and her husband were dating, that further allows us a peek inside the more down-to-earth side of the man: "When my father was given a ride in a car from Boston to Maine, driven by Ed, he said, 'Martha, you cannot possibly marry a person who drives like that!' He thought Ed was the world's worst driver, and I think he was right. My husband was a threat on the highway."

A threat on the highway, maybe — but an indisputable trail blazer in a most remarkable career, whose impact will be felt forever. Salvador Dali once declared that "geniuses never die." Indeed, giants like Dali and Dr. Klein live on forever. Their accomplishments are immortal. One would expect nothing less of guardian angels.

About the Author

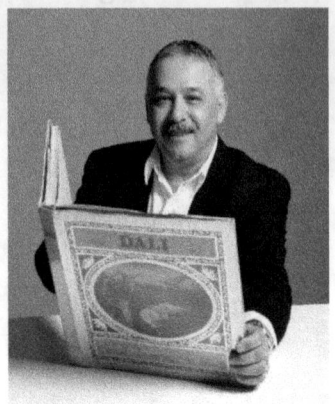

Photo by Bill Wippert

Paul Chimera is an independent journalist, marketing writer, and adjunct professor. He has spent his entire adult life studying the life and work of Salvador Dali, and had the unique pleasure of spending some time with Dali in 1973 and 1974 in New York. He's the former publicity director of the original Salvador Dali Museum of Beachwood, Ohio, and has written extensively on the artist's work. He and his wife Anne reside in Kenmore, New York, a suburb of Buffalo. They have four daughters between them, several grandchildren, and a cat named Elsa.

www.ingramcontent.com/pod-product-compliance
Lightning Source LLC
Chambersburg PA
CBHW060403190526
45169CB00002B/730